MW00451355

THIS JOURNAL BELONGS TO

....

CONTACT
INFORMATION

....

....

....

DATE

....

Battlefield
of the
mind
journal

JOYCE MEYER

FaithWords

New York • Nashville

Copyright © 2023 by Joyce Meyer

Cover design based on *Battlefield of the Mind*, by Joyce Meyer. Cover copyright © 2023 by Hachette Book Group, Inc.

Hachette Book Group supports the right to free expression and the value of copyright. The purpose of copyright is to encourage writers and artists to produce the creative works that enrich our culture.

The scanning, uploading, and distribution of this book without permission is a theft of the author's intellectual property. If you would like permission to use material from the book (other than for review purposes), please contact permissions@hbgusa.com. Thank you for your support of the author's rights.

FaithWords

Hachette Book Group

1290 Avenue of the Americas, New York, NY 10104

faithwords.com

twitter.com/faithwords

First Edition: September 2023

FaithWords is a division of Hachette Book Group, Inc. The FaithWords name and logo are trademarks of Hachette Book Group, Inc.

The publisher is not responsible for websites (or their content) that are not owned by the publisher.

The Hachette Speakers Bureau provides a wide range of authors for speaking events. To find out more, go to hachettespeakersbureau.com or email HachetteSpeakers@hbgusa.com.

FaithWords books may be purchased in bulk for business, educational, or promotional use. For information, please contact your local bookseller or the Hachette Book Group Special Markets Department at special.markets@hbgusa.com.

Unless otherwise noted, the quotes in this book were taken from Joyce Meyer's book *Battlefield of the Mind*. Scripture quotations are taken from the Holy Bible, New International Version®, NIV®. Copyright ©1973, 1978, 1984, 2011 by Biblica, Inc.™ Used by permission of Zondervan. All rights reserved worldwide. www.zondervan.com The "NIV" and "New International Version" are trademarks registered in the United States Patent and Trademark Office by Biblica, Inc.™

Print book interior design by Bart Dawson

ISBNs: 978-1-5460-1251-1

Printed in China

APS

10 9 8 7 6 5 4 3 2 1

Introduction

Learning to think the way God thinks is vital to overcoming negative thoughts that keep us from experiencing the wonderful life Jesus died to give us. The key is to consistently spend time studying God's Word so we know it well enough to determine if what we are thinking lines up with the way God thinks and His thoughts toward us. Second Corinthians 10:5 says that any thought "that sets itself up against the knowledge of God" should be taken captive and made obedient to Christ (NIV).

If you are one of the millions of people who suffer from worry, doubt, confusion, depression, anger, or condemnation, you are experiencing an attack in your mind. But you don't have to live your whole life like this. It's amazing how much your life can change when you realize that you don't have to just accept every thought that comes into your mind.

I pray that recording your thoughts and prayers in this journal, along with my book *Battlefield of the Mind*, will help you firmly establish in your heart forever that you can think the way God thinks by renewing your mind with His Word and lining up your thoughts with His thoughts. It's a process that will bring you into the life of freedom, peace, and joy that God has created you to live!

Our actions are a direct result of our thoughts.
If we have a negative mind, we will have a negative life.

The mind is the battlefield. It is a vital necessity that we line up our thoughts with God's thoughts.

Don't ever give up, because little by little you are changing.

The more you change your mind for the better,
the more your life will also change for the better.

When you begin to see God's good plan for you in
your thinking, you will begin to walk in it.

Changing your way of thinking will enable you to change things in your life that you thought you would have to live with forever.

Prayer is relationship with the Godhead. It is coming and asking
for help or talking to God about something that bothers us.

If you want to have an effective prayer life, develop
a good personal relationship with the Father.

Get to know Jesus. He is your Friend. He died for you. Get to know the Holy Spirit. He is with you all the time as your Helper. Let Him help you.

Learn to fill your prayers with the Word of God.

Our weapons are the Word used in various ways. We can pray the Word, speak the Word, sing the Word, and study the Word.

We need spiritual weapons because we are fighting master spirits, yes, even the devil himself. Even Jesus used the weapon of the Word in the wilderness to defeat the devil.

Our past may explain why we're suffering, but we must not use it as an excuse to stay in bondage.

Jesus always stands ready to fulfill His promise to set the captives free.

God doesn't abandon us and leave us helpless.

God will not allow us to be tempted beyond what we can bear, but with every temptation He will also provide the way out, the escape.

Satan knows well that if he can control our thoughts, he can control our actions.

You may have some major strongholds in your life that need to be broken. Let me encourage you by saying, "God is on your side."

....

....

....

....

....

....

....

....

....

....

....

....

....

....

....

....

....

....

....

....

....

....

....

If we think fleshly thoughts, wrong thoughts, negative thoughts,
we cannot walk in the Spirit. Renewed, God-like thinking is
a vital necessity to a successful Christian life.

One of the best aids to freedom is asking God for
a lot of help—and asking often.

Once I learned that fellowship with Him is vital,
I gave it priority in my life.

Once I realized that right thinking is vital to victorious living,
I got more serious about thinking about what I was
thinking about, and choosing my thoughts carefully.

No matter how bad the condition of your life and your mind, don't give up!

The Holy Spirit is your Helper—seek His help.
Lean on Him. You can't make it alone.

When we begin to feel that the battle of the mind is just too difficult and that we aren't going to make it, then we must be able to cast down that kind of thinking and choose to think that we are going to make it!

There is a war going on, and your mind is the battlefield.
But the good news is that God is fighting on your side.

The renewing of your mind will take place little by little,
so don't be discouraged if progress seems slow.

I believe pride is the "beast" that will consume us
if we receive too much freedom too quickly.

Praise and worship are really battle positions! They confuse the enemy.
When we take our position, we will see the enemy's defeat!

It will definitely take time, and it won't all be easy, but you are going in the right direction if you choose God's way of thinking.

Not only must we choose to think that we are going
to make it, but we must also decide not to quit.

Our thoughts become our words. Therefore, it is vitally important that we choose life-generating thoughts. When we do, right words will follow.

Think good thoughts, and the fruit in your life will be good.
Think bad thoughts, and the fruit in your life will be bad.

Make up your mind that you will not quit and give up until victory is complete and you have taken possession of your rightful inheritance.

You can regain the territory the devil has stolen from you.

Bombarded with doubts and fears, we must take a stand and say, "I will never give up! God is on my side, He loves me, and He is helping me!"

Don't be a quitter! Don't have that old "give-up" spirit.

Whatever you may be facing or experiencing right now in your life,
I am encouraging you to go through it and not give up!

It's easy to quit; it takes faith to go through.

After we have finally decided to be like-minded with God, then we will need to choose and to continue to choose right thoughts.

When we try to do something on our own, fail, and then realize that
we must wait on Him, our hearts overflow with thanksgiving
and praise as He rises up and does what we cannot do ourselves.

God is looking for people who will go all the way through with Him.

Don't receive condemnation when you have setbacks or bad days. Just get back up, dust yourself off, and start again.

When you fail (which you will), that doesn't mean that you are a failure. It simply means that you don't do everything right.

The devil will try his hardest to stop you in this area of renewing the mind.

....

....

....

....

....

....

....

....

....

....

....

....

....

....

....

....

....

....

....

....

....

....

....

....

The way God helps us make spiritual progress is by being with us to strengthen and encourage us to "keep on keeping on" in rough times.

....

....

....

....

....

....

....

....

....

....

....

....

....

....

....

....

....

....

....

....

....

....

....

....

God wants us to be encouraged, not discouraged.

....

....

....

....

....

....

....

....

....

....

....

....

....

....

....

....

....

....

....

....

....

....

....

Think discouraging thoughts, and you'll get discouraged.
Think condemning thoughts, and you'll come under
condemnation. Change your thinking and be set free!

When discouragement or condemnation tries to overtake you, examine your thought life.

God's timing is perfect. He is never late.

I recommend that you not only purposely think right thoughts, but that you go the extra mile and speak them aloud as your confession.

Remember, you become what you think.

We all have to accept the fact that along with
strengths we also have weaknesses.

Positive minds produce positive lives.

I repeat: Don't receive condemnation. Your total victory will come, but it will take time because it will come "little by little."

When our thoughts are negative, everything becomes negative.

Let Christ be strong in your weaknesses; let Him
be your strength on your weak days.

God has a perfect plan for each of us, and we can't
control Him with our thoughts and words.

Begin to think positively about your life.

The pathway to freedom begins when we face
the problem without making excuses for it.

You can have your mind renewed according to the
Word of God. Good things are going to happen to you.

....
....
....
....
....
....
....
....
....
....
....
....
....
....
....
....
....
....
....
....
....
....
....
....
....

I am free to believe that with faith and hope in Him,
the bad things can be turned around for good.

It is unwise to refuse to face reality; however if our reality is negative we can still have a positive attitude toward it.

When the conviction to change comes, ask God to help you.
Don't think you can change yourself. Lean on Him.

Don't ever let evil forebodings hang around in your atmosphere;
instead resist them aggressively in the name of Jesus Christ.

Even though I was extremely negative, God let me know that
if I would trust Him, He would cause me to be very positive.

Pay attention to the condition of your mind
and keep it free, peaceful, and full of faith.

Expect a miracle in your life.

Whatever happens, trust in the Lord—and be positive!

No matter how negative you are or how long you have been that way, I know you can change because I did.

The Word of God teaches us what we should spend our time thinking about.

....

....

....

....

....

....

....

....

....

....

....

....

....

....

....

....

....

....

....

....

....

....

....

....

....

....

How much time do you spend thinking about the Word of God?

The devil was controlling my life because he was controlling my thoughts.

It is very beneficial to think about God's Word. The more time a person spends meditating on the Word, the more he will reap from the Word.

Expect good things!

....

....

....

....

....

....

....

....

....

....

....

....

....

....

....

....

....

....

....

....

....

....

....

....

....

....

....

You should take inventory on a regular basis and ask
yourself, "What have I been thinking about?"
Spend some time examining your thought life.

Let me say it one final time: Think about what you are thinking about. You may locate some of your problems and be on your way to freedom very quickly.

Satan will aggressively fight against the renewal of your mind,
but it is vital that you press on and continue to pray
and study in this area until you gain measurable victory.

You cannot have a positive life and a negative mind.

Recognizing the problem is the first step toward recovery.

If the mind is too busy, it will miss what the Lord is
attempting to reveal to you through your spirit.

The mind should be kept peaceful.

Yet the mind should also be alert. This becomes impossible when it is loaded down with things it was never intended to carry.

The ways of the Holy Spirit are gentle; most of the time
He speaks to us in "a still small voice."

Be serious about tearing down the strongholds Satan has built in your mind. Use your weapons of the Word, praise, and prayer.

The present moment is the greatest gift we have from God,
but if we are not present we miss it.

The Holy Spirit is your Helper—seek His help.
Lean on Him. You can't make it alone.

Wondering, indecision, and confusion prevent an individual from
receiving from God, by faith, the answer to his prayer or need.

As Christians, as believers, we are to believe—not doubt!

I have found out that God wants me to obey Him, whether or not I feel like it, want to, or think it is a good idea.

Reasoning opens the door for deception and brings much confusion.

....

....

....

....

....

....

....

....

....

....

....

....

....

....

....

....

....

....

....

....

....

....

....

....

....

....

....

....

....

When God speaks, we are to mobilize—not rationalize.

Doubt comes in the form of thoughts that are
in opposition to the Word of God.

Satan knows how dangerous we will be with a heart full
of faith, so he attacks us with doubt and unbelief.

The devil brings storms into your life to intimidate you.
During a storm, remember that the mind is the battlefield.

If we know the Word, then we can recognize when the devil is lying to us.

Since you can choose your own thoughts, when doubt
comes you should learn to recognize it for what
it is, say "No, thank you"—and keep on believing!

Don't make your decisions based on your thoughts or feelings, but check with your spirit. When you do, you will find the same vision that was there in the beginning.

It is impossible to have joy and peace and live in unbelief.

....

....

....

....

....

....

....

....

....

....

....

....

....

....

....

....

....

....

....

....

....

....

....

....

....

....

Make up your mind that you will not be
doubleminded; don't live in doubt!

God has a great life planned for you.
Don't let the devil steal it from you through lies!

Worry certainly never makes anything better,
so why not give it up?

Because I was constantly worrying about something,
I never enjoyed the peace that Jesus died for me to have.

....

....

....

....

....

....

....

....

....

....

....

....

....

....

....

....

....

....

....

....

....

....

....

....

....

....

....

Our words are very important because they confirm our faith—
or in some instances our lack of faith.

Satan attempts to steal that life from us in
many ways—one of them being worry.

It is absolutely impossible to worry and live in peace at the same time.

Worry will not help our cause at all. It will, in fact, hinder our progress.

Life is to be lived—here and now!

God's grace is on you to handle whatever you need for today, but tomorrow's grace will not come until tomorrow comes—so don't waste today!

We can choose to be peaceful by choosing to think on things that promote peace rather than things that open a door for worry and anxiety.

The proud man is full of himself, while the humble man is full of God.
The proud man worries; the humble man waits.

....

....

....

....

....

....

....

....

....

....

....

....

....

....

....

....

....

....

....

....

....

....

....

....

....

You and I can pitch or throw our problems to God and, believe me,
He can catch them. He knows what to do with them.

Jesus did not come to remove all opposition from our lives, but rather
to give us a different approach to the storms of life.

....
....
....
....
....
....
....
....
....
....
....
....
....
....
....
....
....
....
....
....
....
....
....
....
....
....

The quality of life that God has provided for us is great enough to provide all of the things we need, but if we worry about the things, then we lose them as well as the life He intended us to have.

....

....

....

....

....

....

....

....

....

....

....

....

....

....

....

....

....

....

....

....

....

....

....

....

We live in a world filled with turmoil. It is around us,
but it does not have to be in us.

Being at peace, enjoying the rest of God in the midst of the storm, gives much glory to the Lord because it proves that His ways work.

When the thoughts being offered to you do not agree with God's Word,
the best way to shut the devil up is to speak the Word.

God knows what we need before we ask. If we will simply
make our requests known to Him (see Phil. 4:6 KJV),
He will bring them to pass in His own good timing.

God met all our needs, and He did it in a variety of ways.
He never let us down—not one time. God is faithful!

Sometimes we are more concerned about telling people what we think than we are about listening, learning, and building good relationships.

Remember, your actions won't change until your mind does.

Be positive and not negative!

Following His way brings fruitfulness;
following the devil's way brings rottenness.

God is the only One Who has the right to condemn or sentence,
therefore, when we pass judgment on another, we are,
in a certain sense, setting ourselves up as God in his life.

If you want to have life flowing to you and from you, guard your heart.

Do your part, but do not try to do God's part. The load is too heavy to bear—
and if you're not careful, you will break under the weight of it.

Each of us belongs to God, and even if we have weaknesses, He is able to
make us stand and to justify us. We answer to God, not to each other;
therefore, we are not to judge one another in a critical way.

The Word coming forth out of a believer's mouth, with faith to
back it up, is the single most effective weapon that can be
used to win the war against worry and anxiety.

Trust and faith bring joy to life and help relationships
grow to their maximum potential.

Always place your ultimate trust in the Lord.

If you want to live the resurrection life that Jesus has provided, then seek that new, powerful life by setting your mind and keeping it set on things above, not on things on the earth.

Words and thoughts are like bone and marrow—so close,
it is hard to divide them (see Heb. 4:12).

Right action begins with right thinking.

The place we give Satan is often empty space. An empty, passive mind can be easily filled with all kinds of wrong thoughts.

All the things that God tries to teach us are for
our own good and happiness.

Start today choosing right thoughts.

Don't be passive in your mind.

Most believers struggle trying to do right, but fruit is not the product of struggle. Fruit comes as a result of abiding in the vine (see John 15:4 KJV). And abiding in the vine involves being obedient (see John 15:10 KJV).

....
....
....
....
....
....
....
....
....
....
....
....
....
....
....
....
....
....
....
....
....
....
....
....

Pray for true gifts—not flesh that masquerades as gifts of the Spirit.

Judgment, criticism, and suspicion never bring joy.

*S*uspicion cripples an entire relationship and usually destroys it.

A passive person may want to do the right thing, but he never will do so unless he purposely activates his mind and lines it up with God's Word and will.

One way to keep wrong thoughts out of your mind
is to keep your mind full of right thoughts.

Begin to operate in the mind of Christ, and you will
step into a whole new realm of living.

It is impossible to get from wrong behavior to right
behavior without first changing thoughts.

Maintain positive thoughts and expectations.
Engage in positive conversation.

Depression oppresses a person's spiritual freedom and power.

....

....

....

....

....

....

....

....

....

....

....

....

....

....

....

....

....

....

....

....

....

....

....

....

....

Think deliberately according to the Word of God; don't just think whatever falls into your head, receiving it as your own thought.

God wants to lift us up, and the devil wants to press us down.

Send thoughts of love toward other people.
Speak words of encouragement to them.

A person flowing in the mind of Christ will find his thoughts
filled with praise and thanksgiving.

Expressing appreciation is not only good for the other person,
but it is good for us, because it releases joy in us.

Every time a negative, condemning thought comes to your mind,
remind yourself that God loves you, that you have been made
the righteousness of God in Christ.

When received by faith, the gift of righteousness will begin
to produce more and more right behavior.

....

....

....

....

....

....

....

....

....

....

....

....

....

....

....

....

....

....

....

....

....

....

....

Have a positive outlook and attitude.